This book belongs to

_____

Characters (in order of appearance)
Narrator   ROY DOTRICE
Belle   PAIGE O'HARA
Beast   ROBBY BENSON
Gaston   RICHARD WHITE
Maurice   REX EVERHART
LeFou   JESSE CORTI
Lumiere   JERRY ORBACH
Cogsworth DAVID OGDEN STIERS

Produced by RANDY THORNTON and TED KRYCZKO

This is a Parragon book
This edition published in 2006
Parragon
Queen Street House
4 Queen Street
Bath, BA1 1HE, UK

ISBN 1-40546-695-2
Manufactured in China

Disney's
Beauty
and
the Beast

p

Once upon a time, a young Prince lived in a shining castle. One cold night an old beggar woman arrived, offering him a single rose in return for shelter from the cold. Repulsed by her ugliness, he turned her away. Suddenly she transformed into a beautiful enchantress.

To punish the Prince, she turned him into a hideous beast. Then she gave him a magic mirror and the enchanted rose, telling him it would bloom until his twenty-first year. To break the spell, he must love another and earn that person's love in return before the last petal fell.

Nearby in a small village, a beautiful young woman named Belle hurried through town. She greeted the townspeople and then rushed to her favourite shop – the bookstore. The owner gave her a book as a gift.

A dreamy look crossed Belle's face. "It's my favourite! Far-off places, daring sword fights, magic spells, a prince in disguise… Oh, thank you very much!"

Belle rushed outside, reading as she walked.

As Belle walked, a handsome hunter named Gaston ran after her. "Belle, the whole town's talking about you. It's not right for a woman to read! It's about time you got your nose out of those books and paid attention to more important things – like me."

Belle tried to get away without being rude, but Gaston's friend LeFou joined them and began to insult her father, an inventor.

"My father's not crazy! He's a genius!" As Belle spoke, an explosion boomed from her father's cottage and she took off running.

At the cottage, Belle found her father and told him what the villagers were saying about her. "They think I'm odd, Papa."

"Don't worry, Belle. My invention's going to change everything for us. We won't have to live in this little town forever!"

Belle's father hitched up their horse, Philippe, and set off for the fair with his new invention. Belle waved. "Good-bye! Good luck!"

But Maurice got lost and accidentally led Philippe into a bleak, misty forest. As he paused to get his bearings, Maurice saw two yellow eyes staring out of the darkness. It was a wolf! Philippe reared and bolted away. Terrified, Maurice ran through the forest with the wolves racing behind him. When he reached a tall, heavy gate, Maurice dashed inside, slamming the gate on the wolf whose sharp teeth snapped at his leg.

Still trembling, Maurice turned to see a huge, forbidding castle. "Hello? I've lost my horse and I need a place to stay for the night."

"Of course, Monsieur! You are welcome here!" Maurice whirled around. There was no one in sight! Then he looked down and saw a mantel clock with a stern, frowning face. Beside him stood a smiling candelabra! Maurice grabbed the clock and examined it. "This is impossible. Why – you're alive!"

The enchantress had also turned all the Prince's servants into household objects. As Cogsworth the mantel clock protested, Lumiere, the candelabra, showed Maurice into the drawing room. There he met a friendly teapot named Mrs Potts and her son, a cute teacup named Chip. Suddenly, the door flew open. A voice boomed. "There's a stranger here…" Maurice jumped out of his chair. In the shadows lurked a large, hulking figure. "Please…I needed a place to stay!"

"I'll give you a place to stay!" The Beast grabbed Maurice and dragged him out of the room.

Back home at the cottage, Belle heard a knock at the door and opened it. "Gaston! What a 'pleasant' surprise!"

"Belle, there's not a girl in town who wouldn't love to be in your shoes. Do you know why? Because I want to marry you!"

"Gaston, I'm speechless! I'm sorry, but… but… I just don't deserve you." As Gaston left he tripped and fell in the mud. When Belle peeked out, she saw that the villagers had gathered in her yard hoping to see a wedding. The vicar and all Gaston's friends saw him humiliated!

After the villagers and a very angry Gaston left, Belle ran outside to feed the chickens. There she found Philippe, alone. "Philippe! What are you doing here? Where's Papa?"

The horse whinned anxiously. Frightened, Belle leaped onto Philippe and returned to the mysterious forest. Soon, they found the castle.

"What is this place?" Belle tried to steady Philippe. Then she saw Maurice's hat on the ground.

Belle hurried inside the gloomy castle and wandered down the vast, deserted corridors.

"Papa? Are you here? It's Belle." No one replied, but Belle didn't know that the Enchanted Objects had seen her.

With joy, Lumiere danced around the mantel clock. "Don't you see? She's the one! She has come to break the spell!"

Without noticing them, Belle continued to search for her father.

Finally, Belle discovered Maurice locked in a tower. "Papa! We have to get you out of there!" Suddenly she heard a voice from the shadows.

"What are you doing here?" Belle gasped. "Please let my father go. Take me instead!"

"You would take his place?"

Belle asked the voice to step into the light and was horrified when she saw the huge, ugly Beast. To save her father, however, Belle agreed to stay in the Beast's castle forever.

The Beast dragged Maurice out of the castle and
threw him into a carriage that would return him to town.
There, the inventor stumbled into a tavern where Gaston
was surrounded by his friends. "Please I need your help!
A horrible beast has Belle locked in a dungeon!"

"Did it have cruel, sharp fangs?" one villager sneered.

Maurice grabbed the man's coat. "Yes! Yes! Will you help me out?"

"We'll help you out, old man." Gaston and his pals tossed the inventor out of the tavern. But Maurice's wild story gave Gaston an idea.

At the castle, Belle nervously followed the Beast upstairs. He paused for a moment. "The castle is your home now, so you can go anywhere you like… except the West Wing."

Belle stared back. "What's in the West Wing?"

"It's forbidden!" Glaring, the Beast opened the door to her room. "You will join me for dinner. That's not a request!"

After the Beast stomped off, Belle flung herself on the bed. "I'll never escape from this prison – or see my father again!"

That night, Belle refused to dine with the Beast. Instead, she crept downstairs to the kitchen. All the Enchanted Objects fed and entertained her. Then Cogsworth agreed to take her on a tour.

Belle halted beneath a darkened staircase. "What's up there?"

"Nothing, absolutely nothing of interest at all in the West Wing.

But when Cogsworth wasn't looking, Belle slipped away and raced up the staircase to a long hallway lined with broken mirrors.

Belle cautiously opened the doors at the end of the corridor and entered a dank, filthy room strewn with broken furniture, torn curtains, and grey, gnawed bones. The only living object was a rose, shimmering beneath a glass dome. Entranced, Belle lifted the cover and reached out to touch one soft, pink petal. She did not hear the Beast enter the room. "I warned you never to come here!" The Beast advanced on Belle. "GET OUT! GET OUT!" Terrified by his rage, she turned and ran.

Belle rushed past Cogsworth and Lumiere as she fled the castle. "Promise or no promise, I can't stay here another minute!"

She found Philippe and they galloped through the snow until they met a pack of fierce, hungry wolves. Terrified, the horse reared and Belle fell to the ground. When Belle tried to defend Philippe, the wolves turned on her, snarling. Suddenly, a large paw pulled the animals off her. It was the Beast!

As Belle struggled to her feet, the wolves turned and attacked the Beast, growling fiercely. With a ferocious howl, the Beast flung off his attackers. As the surprised wolves ran off into the woods, the Beast collapsed, wounded.

Belle knew that this was her chance to escape, but when she looked at the fallen Beast, she could not leave him. "Here, lean against Philippe. I'll help you back to the castle."

Meanwhile, Gaston and LeFou were plotting to have Maurice put into Monsieur D'Arque's insane asylum unless Belle agreed to marry Gaston.

At the castle, Belle cleaned the Beast's wounds and thanked him for saving her life. Later, she was quite surprised when he showed her a beautiful library. "I can't believe it! I've never seen so many books in all my life!"

The Beast smiled for the first time. "Then, it's yours!"

That evening Mrs Potts and the other objects watched Belle read a story to the Beast. They were filled with hope that the Beast and Belle were falling in love.

Gradually, the mood in the castle began to change. Belle and the Beast read together, dined together and played together in the snow. They even had a snowball fight! When Belle watched the big awkward Beast try to feed some birds, she realised that he had a kind, gentle side to him – something that she hadn't seen before. In turn, the Beast began to hope that Belle would begin to care for him. He tidied his room, bathed, and dressed up for the evening. He was overjoyed when Belle taught him how to dance.

That evening, the Beast asked Belle if she was happy.

"Yes. I only wish I could see my father. I miss him so much."

"There is a way." The Beast showed Belle the magic mirror. In it, she saw her father lost in the woods, ill from his search for her. When the Beast saw the unhappy look on Belle's face, he decided to let her go, even if it meant that he would never be human again. Before Belle left, he handed her the magic mirror. "Take it with you so you'll always have a way to look back and remember me."

Heartbroken, the Beast watched as Belle rode off on Philippe. When she found her poor father in the forest, Belle brought him home to their cottage so she could nurse him back to health. But almost as soon as they arrived, a tall, thin man knocked on the door. It was Monsieur D'Arque! He had come to take her father to an insane asylum!

"No, I won't let you!" Belle blocked the way.

LeFou had also convinced the villagers that Maurice was crazy because he was raving like a lunatic about some terrible beast.

Gaston put his arm around Belle. "I can clear up this little misunderstanding – if you marry me. Just say yes."

"I'll never marry you! My father's not crazy. I can prove it!"

Belle showed them the Beast in the magic mirror. "He's not vicious. He's really kind and gentle." Enraged, Gaston shouted, "She's as crazy as the old man! I say we kill the Beast!" The mob of villagers locked Belle and her father in the cellar and stormed the Beast's castle.

As the villagers battled the Enchanted Objects, Gaston forced the Beast onto the castle roof. He clubbed the Beast who didn't even try to resist. "Get up! Or are you too 'kind and gentle' to fight back?"

"Stop!" Chip had helped Belle and Maurice escape from the cellar. When the Beast saw Belle, he grabbed Gaston by the throat. But his love for Belle had made him too human. He let Gaston go and faced Belle. Without warning, Gaston stabbed the Beast in the back! The Beast roared. Gaston stepped back and tumbled off the roof to his death.

Wounded, the Beast gazed at Belle before he collapsed. She ran to him and held him in her arms. "No! Please! I love you!"

Suddenly, the rain began to shimmer. Slowly the Beast opened his eyes and in astonishment, he watched his paws transform into hands. He held them out to Belle. "Belle, it's me!"

Belle hesitated and looked into his eyes. "It is you!" The Prince drew her close and kissed her. Then they watched happily as Cogsworth, Lumiere, Chip, Mrs Potts, and all the other servants once again became human. True love had finally broken the spell, and everyone danced for joy.

Now you have finished reading the story of
Beauty and the Beast, why not sing along
with this magical song from the movie?

Be Our Guest

Music by Alan Menken. Lyrics by Howard Ashman.
Produced by Howard Ashman and Alan Menken
Performed by Jerry Orbach (Lumiere), Angela Lansbury (Mrs. Potts), and Chorus

Lumiere

Be our guest! Be our guest!

Put our service to the test,

Tie your napkin 'round your neck, cherie,

And we provide the rest.

Soup du jour!

Hot hors d'oeuvres!

Why, we only live to serve,

Try the grey stuff, it's delicious!

Don't believe me?

Ask the dishes!

They can sing! They can dance!

After all, miss, this is France!

And a dinner here is never second best,

Go on, unfold your menu,

Take a glance, and then you'll,

Be our guest,

Oui, our guest!

Be our guest!

Beef ragout!

Cheese soufflé!

Pie and pudding "en flambe!"

We'll prepare and serve with flair,

A culinary cabaret!

You're alone and you're scared,

But the banquet's all prepared,

No one's gloomy or complaining,

While the flatware's entertaining,

We tell jokes, I do tricks,

With my fellow candlesticks,

Chorus

And it's all in perfect taste,

That you can bet!

All

Come on and lift your glass,

You've won your own free pass to,

Be our guest!

Lumiere

If you're stressed,

It's fine dining we suggest.

All

Be our guest! Be our guest! Be our guest!

Mrs Potts

It's a guest! It's a guest!

Sakes alive, Well, I'll be blessed!

Wine's been poured and thank the Lord,

I've had the napkins freshly pressed,

With dessert she'll want tea,

And my dear, that's fine with me,

While the cups do their soft shoeing,

I'll be bubbling! I'll be brewing!

I'll get warm, piping hot!

Heaven's sakes! Is that a spot? Clean it up!

We want the company impressed!

We've got a lot to do,

Is it one lump or two for you, our guest?

Chorus

She's our guest!

Mrs Potts

She's our guest!

Chorus

Be our guest! Be our guest! Be our guest!

Our command is your request,
It's ten years since we had anybody here,
And we're obsessed,
With your meal, with your ease,
Yes, indeed, we aim to please.

While the candlelight's still glowing,
Let us help you, We'll keep going.

Course by course,
One by one! 'Til you shout,
"Enough, I'm done!"

Then we'll sing you off to sleep as you digest,

Tonight you'll prop your feet up!

But for now, let's eat up!

Be our guest! Be our guest! Be our guest!

Please, be our guest!